TRIAL
and (Mostly)
ERROR

How To Grow Through What You Go Through

LAURA YOUNG

NEWMAN SPRINGS PUBLISHING
320 Broad Street
Red Bank, NJ 07701

First originally published by Newman
Springs Publishing 2023

ISBN 979-8-88763-307-7 (Paperback)
ISBN 979-8-88763-308-4 (Digital)

Printed in the United States of America

To my past self, who really needed to hear all the content in this book, and my tribe, who has loved me through it all.

Contents

Part 3: How It's Going

Introduction

Maybe it was the moment that I found myself alone in a bar on New Year's Eve while my (first) fiancé was strolling the streets, drunk and incoherent. Or maybe it was when I realized that my life seemed like a revolving door filled with toxic men. Whatever the "aha" moment was, I knew long, long ago that life was fucked up or that I was fucked up—one of the two. Either way, it all boiled down to disappointment and failure—disappointment in myself, disappointment in others, failed relationships, and false hopes. I found myself asking time and time again, "What is wrong with me? Why is my life like this? I try so hard. I am a normal, nice human being. There must be more to life than this!" And there I was, thirty years old and desperately wanting more out of life, tirelessly looking for worth and value in all the wrong places for what seemed like my entire existence.

So, dear friend, before you decide to continue reading past the first two f-bombs, I must tell you that I believe life is a contact sport like a dodgeball game you didn't sign up for but find balls flying at your face, trying to tag you out. I believe that you must have *grit*, passion, and perseverance to not only survive but *thrive* in this life. I intend to help you find your inner warrior through a compilation of life lessons, raw honesty, and hard truths.

The kind of honesty I'm referring to is one that can only come from a woman that found out the hard way how to accept all of herself. I am no expert; I don't have a "life coach" degree. But I think that just makes me even more qualified. I am just a normal woman that has struggled through understanding herself and this wild journey. There are still many nooks and crannies that I have yet to explore within myself and other areas I feel I was forced to master by trial and (mostly) error.

Each chapter is a peek into life circumstances that have helped me learn some valuable lessons along the way. At the end of each chapter, I have a challenge for you. Are you ready to take a hold of your circumstances instead of thinking you're a victim of all this craziness? If so, keep reading.

My prayer is that when you finish this book, you feel a little less alone, a little less fucked up, and a little less stressed about what you're not and discover the courage to be everything you *are* and more.

I hope you enjoy the stories and circumstances in my life that brought me to put this pen on the page. They make up the fabric of my life, my fantastically fucked-up quilt of a life, and maybe some of yours as well.

Part 1

HOW IT STARTED

Let the Chaos Commence

Sometimes when chaos burns
like wildfire around us, we
have no other choice but to
fall in love with the warmth.
—Christopher Poindexter

I have OCD. Don't worry, I've had enough therapy to last a lifetime. If you are not familiar with OCD, it is an anxiety disorder that involves excessive thoughts that lead to repetitive behaviors. Sounds fun, right? It started to affect my daily life visibly when I was in elementary school. My bedtime routine was lengthy and calculated. I had to drink a certain number of cups of water, arrange my ChapStick on my nightstand just right, and lie on my back with my hair tightly tucked behind my head. It's a miracle that I ever fell asleep in that coffin position. I was also very scared that something bad was going to happen to my parents if I didn't perform specific "rituals" until it "felt right" to me.

I remember in middle school, I was watching an *Oprah* episode where some lady was so scared of germs that she bathed in bleach daily and wore white gloves everywhere she went, and that was when I realized, *I think I have that.* My parents—being the proactive, superinvolved humans that they are—sought out help for me. My little life was spiraling out of control, and they were helpless to stop it. I started meeting with the school guidance counselor, but eventually, I needed more support. That came in the form of a professional psychologist named Barb. I will never forget my first session with her. I was probably twelve or thirteen years old, and I had on fake acrylic nails painted blue with white snowflakes for decoration for Christmas. "Why," you ask, "do you remember this?" Because I stared at my nails the entire hour and didn't say a word in true preteen fashion. Eventually, I warmed up to her, and she became my confidant and trusted friend. One of the biggest steps I took with her help was identifying my obsessive thoughts and ranking them on a scale from one to ten. From there, we developed scripts of what I could say to myself to combat the obsessions. The mind certainly is a powerful thing, and I mean that in *both* negative and positive ways. What we say to ourselves is arguably the most important voice of all. Conditioning it to be of service to us and not tear us down is a lifelong challenge worth fighting. We quantified my irrational fears that came with not doing the act (compulsion) to make them go away, which kind of makes me sound like I'm a serial killer. But as with most obsessive thoughts, they are infinitesimal in the large scope of life. For the most part, my thoughts involved germs, the fear of getting sick, or turning the damn light switches on and off a certain number of times. Reading that back to myself, I realize it sounds so sad, and for many years, I struggled on and off in severity.

There is no rhyme or reason for OCD. Some say it is genetic, while some say it comes from trauma or a chemical imbalance. I tend to think it is a combination of the two. When a child or person doesn't know how to cope with anxiety, feelings, trauma, or whatever it may be, they come up with a coping mechanism. That is what OCD was to me and still is. Coping, my friends, is the backbone of how we can deal with what is thrown at us while also *enjoying* the chaos. I guess I should start from the beginning.

I have always had anxiety for as long as I can remember. I was glued to my mom's hip and scared of almost everything. My mom wasn't very warm and fuzzy, which didn't help my innate temperament. She was calculated, scheduled, and organized. There was a time and place for fun, and that was, of course, after we crossed our t's and dotted our i's. She still is, to this day, calculated and organized, with a firm belief in time and place. But I loved her *fiercely*. She was an extension of myself, and I didn't want to be without her. Whenever she wasn't around, the ground felt unsteady.

When I was in fourth grade, my mom suffered a sporadic brain aneurism right there in my living room while watching TV. My dad had to rush her to the ER, and my sister and I woke up to my grandparents instead of Mom and Dad. It was a weird day, and I felt clueless.

That day, my dad picked me up from school. His eyes were red-rimmed, and he didn't have much to say before leaving again to see my mom in the hospital. My aunt took over, tending to dinner and taking care of my sister and me. Do you know the one thing I noticed? Aside from the fact that I had never seen my dad that upset, their bed wasn't made. I had never seen their bed wrinkled and their pillows unfluffed. My mom, the beacon of perfection, wasn't there to hold it all together. My nine-year-old self was internalizing so many things that I didn't even know until I dug back in years later.

We couldn't go see my mom for ten days. She was in the ICU, and it was a miracle that she survived. The doctors said that if she had just taken medicine and gone to sleep, she wouldn't have lived. They did all sorts of brain scans and couldn't find the source of the bleed. It had healed itself—*a miracle*. And wouldn't you know it, she was back in the garden, tending to the weeds, the day after she returned home. After being in a bed for ten days, not walking, her muscle mass dissipated, but she sat on the ground and gardened until she was tired. She was always on the go, even when she was supposed to rest.

In my older years, I am beginning to see that kind of perpetual movement in my life as well. Instead of "being," I am always "doing," which is possibly another coping mechanism whereby I measure the success of my days by how much I can check off my to-do list. Does this sound familiar?

The years to follow were rough for my mom and me. I became a teenager who hated rules, cared more about my friends than my family, and didn't see eye to eye with her at all. We had a sketchy relationship, and my OCD was a lingering battle in the background. This was about the time I started to see Barb. My mom came to a couple of sessions. I hated her. I don't know why. That sounds so bad, and it was. Maybe I was mad that she almost died and was acutely aware that the bed would never have been made had she left us with just dad. My familiar stability was pulled from underneath me, and I couldn't function. I couldn't control the compulsions when the obsessions were there because of my lack of control. It was a double-edged sword.

I have a vivid memory of a particular session with Barb where my mom started *listening* and realized her contribution to some of my unsettled and rebellious behavior. She cried that day. I had never seen my mom cry on my behalf. From that day on, I knew she had worked hard to control her own behavior and watch how my behavior changed as a result.

She couldn't control getting sick. I know that now, but as an impressionable little girl, I learned quickly that what you can't control is scary as hell. I basically have been trying to control everything in my life ever since. It is a losing battle. I tried to control the cleanliness of my home, what I ate, my schedule, what happened to me, my thoughts, and what others thought of me. The worst part was me trying to control others because I could not get a handle on myself. Judging and micromanaging other people is a way to justify our own choices or shortcomings.

In these moments or chapters in our lives where we're perpetually wound up and take our perpetual movement out on others, we are only adding to the pandemonium of the world and our lives. The more you try to control something or someone else, the more you lose, not gain.

It takes a conscious effort to live in the moment and not get wrapped up in tightening the reins on everything in your life. Therapy (a lot of it), yoga, people who let you talk openly about your fears, and taking a damn breath have helped ease my control-freakiness. Yet still, to this day, my type A personality takes over, and I try to multitask my way through it instead of sitting back and riding the wave. I hold on too tight in fear of losing someone I care about.

The expectations and standards we hold for ourselves are suffocating. It's hard, I'll give you that. In a moment of panic, the last thing that you want to do is take a breath and relax. At least for me, the first instinct I have is to fix it or do something that makes me feel better (OCD engage). Sitting in discomfort is one of the hardest things to do, and it took me a lot of years to not do some ritual to ease the worry. There have been times in my life when I have a better handle on it than others. But it is important that everyone finds their "thing"—their way of getting through it. I have found that having people to talk to and trust has been my saving grace. Barb, Jennifer, and Sarah have been the three professional head doctors that have medically contributed to my mental growth. The other people, well, they are in the next chapter.

Your challenge

- What's your thing? What makes you feel centered, alive, and at peace?
- What are you trying to control and failing horribly at? How can you let go and dance in the chaos?

Find Your Tribe,
Love Them Hard

Teachers always say, "There is no stupid question. If you are thinking it, odds are that someone else is as well." Me, well, I always asked. I was the one waving her hand wildly and talking out of turn, answering the question when I wasn't called on, or not letting the teacher finish. (The irony here is that

I became a teacher who had to deal with students like me. Karma is a bitch.) Anyways, the point is that I have always been loud, unfiltered, opinionated, rebellious, inquisitive, and honest—sometimes to a fault. I put my flaws out there before someone can point them out, wildly self-aware (insert eye roll).

I would tell boyfriends things about my past that they never had any business knowing. How many people I slept with? Sure! What else do you want to know? I'm an open book. Geez, what was I thinking?

Some would call it transparency, and others would call it plain stupidity. People don't always receive your flaws kindly, and instead of loving you, they scorn you at the first opportunity. As a result, I carried an enormous amount of guilt for who I was, the choices I'd made, and the things I'd said and done. I *slowly* learned that telling the wrong people your deepest secrets and desires can lead to more dissatisfaction.

It is still an anomaly to me that not everyone cares. Some people simply don't have your best interest at heart even when you think they should. Some will use that information, that weakness, as ammunition to further belittle you. This is a lesson I have learned the hard way repeatedly because I still don't seem to get it. My therapist said that I had a problem with attachment. I expose the most vulnerable parts of me to those I care about, and unfortunately, some do not feel the same way in return and have exploited my feelings, leaving me bleeding and wounded. You too? Okay, good. See? You're not alone already, and its only chapter 2!

I put a lot of weight on my relationships. And it's not just my romantic relationships but all my relationships. I care so much and think humans are so important to living a fulfilling, connected life. *But* sometimes relationships don't work out. What a concept. I don't know where I got the idea that if someone comes into your life and you're inseparable, then that would always be the case. The barometer that I used to determine the temperature of my life was based on the health of my current relationships. What I finally realized is that this method of happiness sucks. Why? Because it is contingent on other people! Happiness is an *inside* job. And you can't control other people, not even for one second, not their loyalty, their love, all of it.

Here's a quick synopsis of my "attachment history."

When I was five, it was my neighbor Chelsea. When I was in elementary, it was Ashley. When I was in middle school, it was Jessica. Sidenote: Middle school is terrible. We should all be cryogenically frozen and come back to high school. Megan and Taryn were my best friends in high school. I loved them, truly. After high school, it was Shannon. We went on to live together a couple of times. Then came college and my main chick, Andrea, who has been my one and only constant friendship post high school. Next up was Erin. We were an unlikely duo, but I could talk to her endlessly. And we had the best humor. Fast forward to adulthood, where I met Kaye while teaching in a fabulously fucked-up school. A perfect pair we were and still are.

These ladies (and a few dudes) have taught me so much. Some good and some not so good. Outgrowing people happens. Some fit your past, and some fit your future. And although heartbreaking at times, it is all a part of your journey.

There has been a lot of trial and error to get the stone-cold pack of weirdos that I call my friends. Luckily, some of the ladies I listed above are still near and dear. But the others are long gone, and some more have filled in.

Present day: I have a group of fierce women, who are flawed and fabulous, that I am beyond blessed to call my friends. Andrea, Kaye, and Melissa, you inspire and support me, and you walk this crazy life by my side day in and day out. You make me better, you make me stronger, and you hold me accountable. Thank God for that because I am known to go off the rails.

I suggest you get some bad-ass bitches to call your own, not the fakes and not the Friday-and-Saturday-night posse, No-no, these are not the real ones. The real ones are the ones who have seen you fall in and out of love and, when you lose hope, help you find it again. These women and I have shared secrets and the "grit" of their lives with me. We can talk about our morning shits and moral issues all in the same breath. The authenticity these ladies bring to the table is unprecedented. They don't pretend to be people they are not. I have no patience for people who pretend they are better, and it's probably because I tried endlessly to keep up and always felt like I fell short.

Everyone has struggles, and everyone messes up. Hiding it does the world a disservice. One of the most important things in my life is having a group of committed gals that tell me like it is, and I do the same for them because the world doesn't need any more people who put on a mask and have surface-level conversations. I always believed that bringing your darkness into the light for everyone to see was being strong and transparent. That is still the case, but that's only with my ladies (and now my husband). Not every Tom, Dick, and Harry need to know your business because, once again, not everyone cares—a lesson well learned.

Your challenge

- Who are your people, your tribe? These are the steadfast group of humans that you call your own.
- What can you do today to hold on a little tighter and cherish those relationships?

Ink Therapy

I got my first tattoo when I was fifteen years old in a trailer park home off an eight-mile road in Detroit. I think that sentence says it all, really. Rebellion runs through my veins naturally. My older, cooler boyfriend knew someone so here I was with a couple of other girlfriends, unbuttoning my pants to get an *Aries* symbol tattooed on my hip. The couch was dirty, and the dude that was the boyfriend or husband of the lady doing the tattooing was staring. Do you think I was phased? Not likely. It wasn't long before my mom discovered it while I was blow-drying my hair in my underwear. I was immediately in trouble and taken to the doctors for HIV blood work. It was negative if you were wondering. My parents' distaste for my bad decisions throughout life saved me in so many ways. If it wasn't for their constant involvement, I would be in another place entirely. So my advice here is to listen to your parents, and also, don't listen to your parents.

For my next tattoo, I was smarter and consulted my mom. I carefully picked an artist I loved that made fairy art. My mom took me to a shop, where I met Ryan, the tattoo artist that has since tattooed me countless times over the last nineteen years. Ryan has always had a way of bringing my experiences and thoughts to fruition and turning them into art, and I will forever thank him for this talent. The fairy tattoo was, of course, placed on my lower back. Where else do you get a tattoo when you're eighteen? It was done right before senior spring break where I wore it with pride! I loved that tattoo; it was beautifully done. The next one was marked by the story below.

Besides my mom's near-death experience, I have had two notable traumas in my life. Although there have been others (as my shrink tells me, it is all a matter of perspective), the normal population would agree that these two are for the books. Two of my boyfriends passed away, the first when I was twenty and the second five years later, when I was twenty-five. I know what you're thinking: *What in the actual fuck?* Yeah, me too. Even all these years later, I still think the same thing. Loss is a lot to process, especially with two almost synchronous losses in a five-year span at an impressionable age. But these were the cards I was dealt, and in many cases, beauty comes out of the other end of tragedy. Luckily, in my case, I am proud to say that I am better, stronger, and more self-aware because of these tragedies.

Justin and I went to high school together, but he was a year older than me. Although we didn't know each other then, we met a couple of years after at a party. His friend group was rough around the edges, but I liked that they never made me feel judged. They drank and did drugs, while I was on the dance team and got As in school. But I felt accepted quickly, and Justin and I were soon dating. And this group became my friends.

I was a sophomore in college when I transferred back home to a local university from a school a few hours away.

I became better friends with a high school friend, Shannon, once I returned home. We decided to get an apartment together. We partied a lot and thought we were adults. All the while, I was just learning how to brown meat to make spaghetti. Real-life adults, I tell ya.

Justin's uncle owned an apartment complex in Southwest Detroit, in Mexican Village. Justin moved there to help manage it, aka keep the crime at a dull roar. It was a very dangerous building and area, and I was not by any means affected. Was I naive or stupid? I would say both. His apartment was the penthouse, and we could sit on the roof and see the whole city—the one beautiful thing in all of this.

We dated for six short months when he died. As I type this, I still think it sucks. Justin had some issues with depression. He had a tumultuous relationship with his father. And his grandparents mostly raised him. His mother lived in North Carolina and had two more young children. He and his mom didn't have much of a relationship as far as I know, so it was a surprise when he said he was going to visit her for a week or two. He was there only three days…

I had moved back in with my parents at this point and we were rocky before he left. He would say things like he didn't deserve me or that I shouldn't care about him. If you refer to my earlier writing about attachment issues and trying to fix, help, and heal everything in my path, you'd know that I stuck around.

On the days before he left, he wanted to go to downtown Detroit with Shannon and her boyfriend for a nice dinner and date. We got dressed up and went out to eat, and then we visited the sign dedicated to the family business that has been in business since 1888 when his ancestors came from Germany. We also rode the people mover because he said that he did that with his dad when he was little. I wasn't used to seeing him so excited and smiley. He spent his Christmas money treating us that night. I remember thinking he could have used that money on some new winter clothes. Now I know why he wouldn't need any clothes moving forward.

When I talked to him on the phone on the third night, he was in Carolina, and he told me that his mom gave him some Xanax the night before to help him sleep and that he fell asleep in the bathtub. I was angry and disappointed that he had done that and that his mom had to wake him up while he was naked in the tub at twenty-one years old. I had to go to class in the morning, so I ended the conversation somewhat irritated. When I woke up to my phone buzzing, I answered it while half asleep. It was not him. It was his mom screaming bloody murder, saying that I had killed her son.

The days that followed were a blur. After putting together the events of the short time he was there, to spare you the details, Justin died of carbon monoxide poisoning. He left me a message on my cell phone right before he passed.

It was a long time before I could get rid of that voice mail—a metaphor for my lifelong battle of letting go. I listened to it to hear his voice and his last words even though it was sick and twisted. Maybe I did it to punish myself or remind myself of the pain. The saddest part is that his siblings saw him that morning—a scene I could never imagine and that will be engrained in their minds for eternity, just like that voice mail is to me.

I honestly believe that he went away because no one would have left him alone long enough to do it here. Or maybe it was a big fuck-you to his mom. I will never know. What I will make a point of saying is that Justin wasn't much different from any of his friends. He was struggling with drinking and dabbling in drugs, came from a semibroken home, and was wondering what life would have in store for him. Many would say, "That's just Justin." Such a dangerous thing to brush off. My public service announcement is to always err on the side of caution. Pay attention because burying someone you care about is the worst emotional pain we experience on this earth.

Why am I telling you this? Because the wake of that tragedy has settled. But the waves still ripple through aspects of my life and personality. Wounds heal in some ways, but one tiny pick at a scab can open the whole sore. I have his initials tattooed on my ankle. I also have on my ribs the initials of the other boyfriend who passed, as well as cherry blossoms to signify the fragility and brevity of life. Many would say to never do such a thing, but I never regretted it. Those initials have meant different things at different times since that day. When people say, "I could never get a tattoo. I wouldn't know what I want permanently on me," I am reminded that the things we carry through this life are with us permanently no matter if we wear them on our skin or in our hearts. I choose to wear it on my skin and be proud of the puzzle pieces that make up who I am.

Since then, I have gotten a variety of tattoos, each in different seasons of my life. I have had some covered up, some redone, some done with a lot of thought, and others done on a whim. I look at each one of them and see my past self in them. I see marks of pain, beauty, and growth. My latest ones are birth flowers for each of my three kids. Whatever your therapy, your history, or your processing technique, I simply think you should have one because the statement you can make without apologies is absolutely the one you should make.

Your challenge

- What are you hiding from the world because of fear—fear of what people might say or think, fear of your truth, or fear of what might happen?
- What tragedy have you let eat at you for years that you desperately want to make a part of your story but not the whole thing?

An excerpt from my journal written on December 11, 2006

> I no longer have your pictures up in my room. I don't read your poem or look at my picture book of you. All your things are in a box in my basement. I am sooo sorry. I am so sorry I

couldn't help you while you were here. I am so sorry I didn't wake up to your phone call. I'm sorry I didn't do more that night to save you. That I didn't do more ever. I'm sorry I haven't written until now. I love when you come to see me in my dreams. I love to talk to you in my dreams and for that moment you exist all over again. For that moment you talk to me and smile at me. Come more often. Come every night. Come tonight. It's crazy when I think about you it seems so unreal. Help me to be happy and remember your smile when those thoughts come. I promise to never forget you. I could never. God put you in my life for a reason whatever it was I am ok with. I trust him. I just wish I knew more. I wish I knew what you were thinking; what was so wrong; what happened at your mom's house. I wish I'd known how to save your life. I don't know if the pain or guilt will ever subside. Until next time, Laura.

Justin Lee Hesse:
May 16, 1984–February 2, 2006

Roots and Wings

I'm more Armenian than the Kardashians. Yeah, I said it! Their dad was 50 percent Armenian, making them a quarter each. My dad is 100 percent Armenian, making me—you guessed it—50 percent! I don't have the ass, duck lips, or plastic surgery they do, but I do have more body hair than the average gal. I have that going for me at least. I have three boy cousins that are 50 percent Italian and 50 percent Armenian. They have a five-o'clock shadow by noon. My dad (Jerry) is one of six kids. He is the oldest boy with four sisters before him (Joyce, Jean, Mary, and Diana).

Every single Sunday of my childhood was spent at my grandmother's house in Romeo, Michigan, at her pool and with my whole family. And when I say *my whole family*, I mean my whole freaking family. When I think back to my most vivid memories, this is by far at the top of my list. As an adult now with kids of my own, I can wholeheartedly appreciate the effort, love, and commitment to spend a whole day of your weekend somewhere away from home. We swam all day until our feet bled. The pool was concrete, and we had to wear socks while swimming so they wouldn't get annihilated. We would have raft races and try to dive to the bottom of the ten-foot-deep pool to feel our ears pop. My uncle David sweat his ass off while grilling and then dove in right before we ate. Dessert was always watermelon, the veggies were all from my grandmother's garden, and my grandmother cleaned a chicken bone like no one I'd ever seen.

I grew up knowing that I was Armenian and eating my grandmother's cooking on Sundays. This included pilaf, chi kofte, lahmajun, lamb, baklava, dolma, and apple pie. So. Much. Apple. Pie. Fun fact: When she passed away, we ate apple pie for an entire year. That's how many freezers with food the woman had in her basement. It must be where I get the freezer-prep mindset from!

None of my family members can speak Armenian, although I desperately wish they did! My dad said that his parents spoke Armenian to each other but not to the children because they were "American." I'm sure they felt they were truly living the American dream after sustaining some terrible hardships. Unfortunately, I never met my grandfather, but I really wish I knew him and his history firsthand because there are so many things we do not know about him.

The little that we do know about my grandfather was taken from an interview of him that was published of him as a town business owner in the *Romeo Observer* newspaper. Sarcus (Sam) Varvarian was born in July 1908 in Armenia and had six siblings. He lived a short seven years before his family was massacred during the Armenian genocide in 1915. If you haven't seen the movie *The Promise,* you should. The Armenian genocide was denied for over one hundred years as ever happening. At least 1.5

million Armenians were deported and massacred in the Ottoman Empire (modern-day Turkey). As far as we know, none of his family survived this atrocity, or they were separated beyond trace. He was adopted by a Turkish family where he suffered abuse until he escaped to an orphanage six hundred miles away. Later, the children of the orphanage were moved to Constantinople and then Greece. The first glimmer of hope came from a friend in the orphanage that had conversations with a family member in New York and helped with arrangements for him to come to America.

He first arrived in Canada at the ripe age of sixteen years old, and two years later, America. Niagara Falls was his first stop and, coincidentally, also the location of my grandparents' honeymoon. In 1927, he arrived in Detroit and worked at Ford as a tool grinder for seventeen years. He also worked odd jobs, mostly in restaurants. With frequent layoffs at Ford, he ended up working part-time at friend's shoe store. It was about this time where he met my grandmother, and they were married on October 26, 1941, through an arranged marriage. My grandmother was only twenty-one years old at the time and told me she was devastated and even had a boyfriend at the time she was promised to my grandfather. She said she locked herself in the closet on her wedding day, but my grandfather was gracious and patient. She told me she obviously fell in love with him because they had six children. I remember thinking, *Grandma! Gross!* when she told me that.

My grandmother was also born in Armenia but on January 15, 1920. She had three siblings: two sisters (Mary and Sevart) and one brother (Albert). Her parents were married in 1919. She was born a year later, and when she was two years old, they immigrated to America. It seems they first settled in Connecticut, where her next two siblings were born. They settled on a farm in Romeo, and my dad and his siblings at least knew/know that side of the family. Her parents, Minus (John) Shanlian and Tamon (Thelma) Sapsuzian, owned the Romeo Café in Romeo, Michigan.

Two years into their marriage, my twin aunts (Joyce and Jean) were born. And not long after that, the opportunity to buy a shoe store came about, and they jumped on it. They owned Sam's Shoes in Romeo for thirty-eight years and were also proud and successful members of the community and members of the Methodist church. Sadly, my grandfather died at his desk of a heart attack in the shoe store at only fifty-nine years old. As a mother, I have no idea how my grandmother continued to work full-time, running the shoe store and raising six kids. My grandma told me she went to parent-teacher conferences for thirty-six years straight. What in the actual fuck? I cannot even imagine the daily grind that had to take place to clothe, feed, and bathe six humans, especially as a widow.

My grandmother died in 2004 of a brain hemorrhage. She golfed and cooked until the day she died. We were all very fortunate to be able to see her lucid and joking with us before she passed peacefully in the hospital. She was the glue and backbone of our family and is truly missed. It is a good thing my aunts cook all the Armenian food still at our family gatherings, because without that, I think a lot of our traditions would be lost.

The value of family is a *huge* part of who I am and who I want to be. Writing my history is therapeutic to me because knowing where I come from helps me stay grounded and find solace in the memories. It makes me want to provide the same for my children. Isn't it true that we need to know where we came from to know where we're headed? Either you want to replicate pieces of your past, or you want to do the exact opposite. And to be honest, the pieces will follow you, the good or the bad. They pop up in our personalities, and we get to make the decision of whether it is a piece we want to keep or discard.

I recently heard a quote that said, "The family you are building is more important than the family you came from." I can see what they're saying. Although my immediate and extended family shaped me, supported me, and have known me my whole life, my immediate family is now my husband and the little humans we have made together. I am equal parts responsible for taking all the good and recreating it and taking all the not-so good and breaking the cycle.

As a parent now, I can create traditions of our own, ones that my kids will look back on and remember, like my Sundays spent at my grandmother's or family vacations. But at the same time, I am painfully aware of how much time, effort, and consistency it takes to create memories and experiences for your kids. A few special ones that I remember from my childhood are around the holidays. We'd always have eggs, sausage, and coffee cake on Christmas morning before we were allowed to open our stockings. We also would light an Advent-calendar candle each week leading up to Christmas, and my mom had this little passage she'd read at dinner. For Lent, we were challenged to give something up or take something new on. We spent the Fourth of July up at our family cabin with neighbors that I consider family. I've never missed a summer in my thirty-eight years of life. Now I take my kids there each summer, and the new generation better become besties. I attended church camp each summer from the age of four to my senior year of high school. My grandma always made a "Happy Birthday, Jesus" cake at Christmas, and we would sing "Happy Birthday" to him. Even simpler, we'd eat dinner together every night, and my mom sang me to sleep.

I hope my kids remember the big and small things that we do as parents to make their lives fulfilling, fun, and full of purpose. I am thankful to my parents for taking the time to create traditions I cherish and the courage to establish my own.

Your challenge

- What are some of your favorite childhood memories that you had as a family?
- Are there traditions you want to keep, and are there ones you would rather not?
- Think about childhood from your kids' eyes for a minute. Is it what you want them to remember and experience?

Part 2

HOW IT WENT

Well-Behaved Women
Barely Make History

The rebel in me will never die.
              —James Davis

I have always considered myself the black sheep of the family. I knew the rules but lived by the philosophy "Do first and ask for forgiveness later." My sister, on the other hand, believed that rules were important and there for a reason. Whatever the reason was, the reason was dumb as far as I was concerned. I fought tooth and nail with my parents from sixth grade onward. I pushed the envelope in every way—curfew, phone privileges, sleepovers, the guys I dated, where I wanted to go, and what I wanted to wear. I smoked my first cigarette and got felt up in middle school. Dad, if you are reading this, please go to the next chapter.

By the time I was sixteen years old, I lost my virginity on an air mattress in some random house I had never been to. Remember that boyfriend that took me to the trailer park for my first tattoo? Yep, you called it. It was he who I decided would be the guy to lose my virginity to. And so began my journey of questionable dating and decisions.

I still stand by my belief in questioning authority. Never blindly agree or follow someone just because they are in a position of power. Power and leadership are two very different things. Be careful whom and what you give power to. Three things I gave too much power to over the years are men, relationships, and people. I gave them the power to change how I feel about myself and my worth—something that took me *years* to overcome and understand.

It is crazy how much men and relationships can have an impact on a young woman's emotional health, which makes me scared for all the young ladies growing up in this day and age especially. I have friends who formed serious relationships in, say, eleventh and twelfth grade. They lost their virginity consensually and with much thought to their boy-friend, who also lost their virginity to them. Then they continued to date and had an amicable breakup before leaving for different colleges. Like, what? This would have been great and not at all damaging to my self-esteem, body image, self-worth, and confidence. But that was *not* my story, and the consequences still run deep.

I left pieces of my soul on each of those beds with each of those (mostly) undeserving men. I felt disgusting, shameful, and unhappy a lot of the time over a span of ten to fifteen years. Often I felt used up and tossed into the trash, where I felt like I belonged anyway. I tried to ground myself, write in my jour-nal, go to church, and have higher standards, but nothing worked.

I made so many excuses for dudes to treat me poorly and ultimately for me to treat myself poorly: "They came from a rough upbringing, "They just didn't see it the way I saw it"—you know, the usual denial. Should I really give up a three-year relation-ship because of one bad decision on their part? The answer should have been *yes*! Yes, Laura, yes, you should say goodbye to the guy that cheated on you after three years of dating and living together, just to give you an STD. Yes, you should break up with the guy who punished you for "having an attitude" by leaving you stranded without a car. Yes, you should stop talking to the guy who only calls you back at 11:00 p.m. to come over, sleep with you, and then leave. Yes, you should never call back the guy who wants to keep you a secret, who won't be your date to anything, or who won't introduce you to anyone. *No*, these men didn't love you. *No*, they didn't have the capacity or maturity to be honest, faithful, and kind. This had nothing to do with you and everything to do with them. Whewww, it felt good to write that. People say that to you, ya know? That it's not you; it's them. But when you're in it, it sure feels like it's you, doesn't it? That something must be wrong with you. There's nothing wrong with you other than you ignoring red flags that I know you can *feel* somewhere deep down.

I constantly thought, *Maybe if I tried harder, they'd see how awesome I am. Maybe if I explained how hurt they made me feel and upped the guilt trip, they'd open their eyes to what is right in front of them.* I tried everything, folks: kindness, patience, understanding, extravagant gifts, and endless excuses. I tried making myself small to make them big. But you know what? Dulling your light to make someone else shine never is a good idea. That rebel in me, that inner fire, never simmered under the surface for long.

I think you always know in your gut when something isn't right, like when someone isn't in your corner and is doing you dirty (I mean, except for the boyfriend that gave me the STD; that one came out of the left field). Eventually, I would put up a fight, say my peace, try to hurt them back, and stand up for myself. But most of the time, I was acting on an equally immature playing field and would end up self-sabotaging instead of walking away peacefully. If I loved myself more, maybe I would have attracted better circumstances. Or maybe I would have just not made it such a long and treacherous road to disengagement.

In a recent conversation with a younger colleague, I found myself so grateful to be out of the dating scene and with a faithful, honest man. My husband does not lack in past mistakes. We have that in common, just in different ways. One thing I do know is that he is the same man in front of me as he is when I'm not around. He is humble and quick to apologize. He sticks around even when things are tough, and I can trust him with however I feel. I hope he loves my "spunk," because that isn't going anywhere.

It took a lot of years, a lot of therapy, and a lot of self-reflection to crawl my way out of that self-loathing ditch. I spent a good fifteen years of my life trading away my body, feelings, and values for approval, acceptance, or both. It was all so demeaning and got me nowhere but lost and longing.

You would think that my advice in this chapter would be to love yourself and say no to anything right away that disrespects and demeans you, but it's not. I want you to do what you think you need to do. Don't let anyone make you feel bad for sticking out of a bad situation until you are *ready* to move on (I mean, unless you are getting physically abused, then leave that hellhole immediately and find help.) But if you need to give someone or something everything you've got or exhaust options so you can look back and be satisfied, then do that! The only thing I ask is that you *learn through what you go through*. What's that one quote? "Mistakes are repeated until learned from"? Yep, that's the one. I should patent that. Remember that. So do the rebellious thing and give them another chance if you need to, but remember that nothing changes if nothing changes. And that ball is in your court.

Your challenge

- What is a mistake you are holding on to from your past that you need to let go of? Can you look back on it with more understanding and less self-judgment?
- Who or what are you giving too many chances to? Is it hurting or helping you? Think about that honestly and then set a boundary to move on.

The Chicken or the Egg?

Needs are imposed by nature.
Wants are sold by society.
—Mokokoma Mokhonoana

"What came first?"—the age-old question. As I mature in years and level of introspection, I wonder what affects us more, nature or nurture—a conversation Kaye and I articulate a lot. I will say that just like everything else in life, it's a balance of both. Thank God for nurture because without my upbringing, I think my nature would have steered me in a whole other direction. As a parent, I understand how one single moment, one single decision, can change the trajectory of your life forever, like being in the wrong place at the wrong time, surrounding yourself with the wrong people, or simply giving in to the less-desirable human qualities, like lust and greed. As a child, I thought, *Ehh, how bad could it be?* The sense that everything is reversable or fixable is a risky domain in the teenage mind. Luckily for me, the wrong turns were just innocent enough to lead to better outcomes, not to mention the tremendous amount of forgiveness and love my parents showed me.

If you ask my dad what the biggest difference between my sister and me is, he'll tell you a story about when I was nineteen years old and living in an apartment with my best friend; I was commuting to college and drinking a ton of Jägermeister on the weekends. We got the cops called on us because of the noise, and we all got "minor in possession" (MIP) charges. Instead of being remorseful, I was full of anger. They had the audacity to come into my home like they owned the place. I was more concerned about the "invasion of privacy" and my "rights" than the laws I was breaking. My sister, on the other hand, was away at college with a responsible designated driver when a gathering got busted. She was underage, with the one beer she drank in her hand. She called home at 2:00 a.m., beside herself with guilt and remorse. There it is. That sums it up: the combative one that has a problem with authority and the remorseful one who keeps her hands clean and follows the rules.

I proceeded to get one more MIP before turning twenty-one, and I had to go to court multiple times and take Breathalyzer tests daily. When I was in court for one such bad decision, the judge told me to turn around and look at the rows of seats. My dad was crying. The judge told me I was lucky to have someone who cared about me enough to come and even luckier to have someone who loved me so much. I cried. I was not a monster; I just got caught up. And the same goes for so many young people who end up in the system without money, support, or better circumstances. The system doesn't care if they just suspended your license; you still must find a way to show up on time for court, take Breathalyzer tests, and work so you can maybe afford the bill they throw at you. Without people on your side, how the hell are you supposed to do that? That's a societal flaw I could write a whole other book about.

My husband's story is not mine to tell, but I will say he climbed his way out of some gnarly circumstances; he lost money, friends, and most of all, his business. He started over as a sober man with no help from the system, that's for sure, just help from a couple of solid-hearted people who loved him dearly.

Mistake number 1,203,486,297, which is worth a mention, also had to do with alcohol. I had graduated and was a professional adult when I got my DUI. It was a Friday night after a long week of teaching, and I met my parents for dinner at a local restaurant and bar. I didn't eat much and was chatting away about something. Surprise, surprise. My friend Eric met us after dinner, and we all listened to live music and drank more. My dad was taking my car and leaving me with my mom's car because he was going to take my car in to get new tires the following day. My helpful, awesome father. He made Eric promise to get my ass home safe. But in good form, when it was time to leave, I was too drunk to drive; and despite Eric's efforts to get me in his car, I refused. All I wanted was my own bed and my mom's car parked at my house, where it was supposed to be. He said he'd follow me, but I pulled out too fast and lost him.

Here's the kicker. My lights usually turned on automatically in my car, but in my mom's, they did not… So I was driving with no lights, and once I hit the main road, I was pulled over and taken in.

The only phone number I knew by heart was my sister's, so I called her after I was fingerprinted and given the phone. She barely said hello before handing the phone to her husband, who proceeded to rush to my rescue with bail money. They wouldn't let me go because I had to be sober to be released, and after blowing *well above* the legal limit, that was going to be a while.

There I was, in a disgusting cell with a metal toilet and a thin-ass blanket, heart racing, and this time, remorse and disgust with myself quickly set in. I could have hurt someone. I could've hurt myself, ended life as I knew it. I called my parents in the morning, and my mom answered cheerfully, stating she was at the farmers market. Telling them I was in jail and that her car was impounded was the worst thing that I had to tell them thus far in my life. Once they picked me up, I immediately puked and bawled my eyes out. My dad was so mad he couldn't even look at me. My mom was crying and holding my hair while I vomited. To say I spent the rest of that day in bed, in a self-loathing state, would be an understatement. I realized at that moment that I was down a bad path of self-destruction. I not only disappointed my parents, but now I was also disappointed in myself. This narrative wasn't what I wanted for myself.

My license got suspended for ninety days except for driving myself to and from work. I had to take Breathalyzer tests randomly also. It cost over ten thousand dollars when all was said and done, but it also humbled me immensely. This was all in the wake of losing Brandon and a wicked spiral of self-loathing and low esteem.

My parents never gave up on me. They would show up to help me rake leaves or mow my lawn, invite me over for dinner, and encourage me the best way they knew how. Although I had always been consistently into fitness, I also quit smoking and started running. In the next couple of years, I completed a half marathon alongside Kaye, who almost had to drag me across the finish line. Slowly but surely, I was weeding out the past, the bad seeds in my life, and focusing on myself and the people who didn't want to just take from me but also give.

I think lessons are repeated until we learn, and our nature and nurture collide along the way. I also think God tried warning me with some soft offenses before slamming the door on my face and telling me to get my shit together. The six years I spent living alone in my small rented house were the most formative of my early adulthood. It was hard for me at first. I hated being alone. I felt like everyone was happier than me and had a partner to lean on. My two best friends were married, and I wasn't even dating anyone seriously. (When I say *seriously*, I mean I was dating everyone, if you know what I mean.) Eventually, I sat with myself long enough to really get through the mud of my inner demons. Don't get me wrong. The path of getting there was messy. I revisited closed relationships that should have stayed in the past, got way too intoxicated, and took scraps from men that didn't deserve my time or energy. *But* I got there. I changed careers and met my husband, Kris. I started to worry more about what I thought rather than what *other* people thought. I set boundaries that I never had the strength to uphold in the past.

A lot can change in a short time, and within five years, I was married with two children and a family to call my own. It is bonkers to see what I used to dream about coming true. I don't give much meaning to some of the things that used to hold me back. It really is just that, isn't it? Two people can have the same experience, and one can think of it as a blessing, a lesson that forged their trajectory forward. Or they can see it as a debilitating part of who they are. You are *wildly* capable of creating the life you want. It takes small choices, a whole lot of *grit,* and being brutally honest with yourself as well as setting boundaries. It takes time, and there is no end date. We are constantly a work in progress, forging toward progress over perfection. Keep on keeping on. If you're not failing, you're not even trying.

Your challenge

- What are you giving too much meaning in your life? How is it holding you back from the life you dream of?
- What part of your nature and your nurture can you celebrate?
- What other people think of you is none of your business. What you think of yourself is what really matters. Are you being kind to yourself?
- Are you choosing to participate in things that don't make you happier, healthier, or wealthier or free up your time? If it's what's expected of you

Dying Sucks, So Write a Will

April 26, 2010, six days after my twenty-fifth birthday, was the day that my life would change once again. Boyfriend number 2 was dead; and I was left feeling hollow, abandoned, and cursed and left with an odd sense of déjà vu.

Brandon and I met through friends, and I was completely into him. I was on the last leg of a serious relationship when we met. We hit it off easily, and I was impressed by his maturity, patience, and gentle nature.

He owned his own home, cooked me dinners, and opened my car door. My favorite memory of Brandon was from Valentine's Day. He had me over, and when I arrived, dinner was cooked; he was wearing an apron, for goodness' sake! Candles were lit, and it was delicious. Then he had sprinkled rose petals down the hallway to the bedroom, with a gift of chocolate-covered strawberries and a scarf waiting on the bed. It was so sweet and thoughtful. Later I learned that he called his mom to bring over candles in a hurry before I arrived because he didn't have any. It was so cute that it still makes me smile. We only dated for a short time, but looking back, our relationship was something that could have disrupted the pattern of my past.

April in Michigan can be a wild card when it comes to weather. This day was the first warm, sunny day we had seen in months. Brandon had gone home for lunch that day to get his motorcycle and take it for a ride since it was so nice out. He was less than a mile from home when he turned out onto a main road from his subdivision and was hit by a man simply going to lunch. He was only going twenty miles per hour and was dead on contact.

I had seen him less than twenty-four hours before his passing, spending the evening planning when we could see each other next during a busy workweek. I was in my first year of teaching and on my way home from work when I got a hysterical phone call from Shannon telling me the news. It was a horrific moment when I realized, *This is really happening.* I had to pull over on the side of the highway and try to stop the world from spinning around me. Oddly enough, my best friend, Andrea, was driving behind me because she had met me after work to pick something up. *Thank God* she was there because I left my body for a short while. I vaguely remember her talking on the phone to my parents and pulling into their driveway.

Sitting on their couch, trying to piece the events together, I laughed. This couldn't be happening *again*, right? But it was, and there was no way out but through. This time around, the denial phase of grief didn't last long.

Grief is a giant. It changes you. It makes you question everything, makes you angry, and makes you feel things you never thought you could or ever wanted to. But it also enhances the human experience. How blessed was I to have loved someone so much that I could feel a loss so deep? That's how I look at it now. This quote I read rang so true after my experiences with loss: "Grief is the last act of love we have to give to those we loved. Where there is deep grief, there was great love."

The hardest thing, I think when looking back, was that the world didn't stop for my grief. I woke up the day after; looked around; and thought, *Here these people are, just going about their day, driving to work, fighting with their spouse, grocery shopping, etc. Don't they know my world was just turned upside down?* I was angry at strangers that could have a normal day. Anger—that's the second stage of grief.

People don't like to talk about death. Many times, the most uncomfortable things are the most important to confront. Loss is messy for the people left on this planet to clean up. Brandon owned his own home, had one payment left on his motorcycle, and had a side business with a friend. He didn't have a will, so his family was left with the probate court and guessing. I wasn't his wife, so people didn't know how much to include me or not include me in the proceedings. Everything was awkward, and feelings ran so high. It wasn't long after this that I wrote my own will. I detailed what was important to me and what I wanted to come of my passing. I gave that document to Andrea along with all my passwords. The funny thing is that she didn't even blink an eye. My girl, she knows me so well. Now I am married with children and had to go to a lawyer for a legit will. I am glad to have people in my life that I can trust in a time of tragedy: my husband, my sister, my parents, and my girls. They got my back, and I know it. They also know what they mean to me and how much I love them and appreciate all the bad decisions, mental breakdowns, and struggles they have seen me through and pulled me out of.

My advice here is to leave nothing unsaid. If it's in your heart, then say it to the people you love. Let them know how much they mean to you and what you want in case something catastrophic happens. Trust me, you don't want to be leaning over your loved one's casket, telling them things you should have said when they had breath in their body. Be obnoxious, call too often, send the gift, take the trip, and spend the time. It is a life lesson I have heard over and over, but we could always use a reminder, preferably not during a loss.

Your challenge

- What could you say today to someone to make a difference and let them know what they mean to you?
- Are you estranged from someone that you could make amends with? Life is too short, my friend. Mend that shit and move on.

Saving the World Isn't Our Job, Although We Should Try

Teachers are a gift from God. Seriously, they're a straight-up hand-wrapped gift from the big man upstairs. When I was in college, I really had no idea of the array of careers out there. I just sort of looked at the major fields: law, medicine, psychology, education, business, engineering (I couldn't even tell you the types of engineering), some sort of office secretary job, and I don't even know what else. My junior and senior years were spent applying to colleges, going to visit them, and writing essays to explain why they should pick me and my brain out of the millions of other applicants. None of my other friends were going away. A couple of them went to a university within commuting distance, and others went to beauty school. Some moved out of state, and others attended simple community colleges. I chose the university both of my parents attended, which was about two and a half hours away. I soul-searched for what I wanted to do. Working at *Hooters* sounded appealing, but I certainly didn't have the body or boobs to sustain that job. I also would have been happy with just existing with my older, cooler boyfriend and taking it from there. But in the end, forensic psychology was my pick. I had shadowed a police officer in Detroit during my senior year, and it was exhilarating. I wanted to become a detective and eventually be a psychologist in a woman's facility. What I found out was that I am a pussy. If someone was apologetic, even a criminal, I would probably believe them. I wouldn't be a good cop by any means. I liked my psychology classes but quickly learned that I would have to do a lot of schooling to make a living, and that was a no-go for me.

When I transferred home after my first year, I had to take an entrance exam for writing and math to get into the new university. I had always been good at math. I tested in calculus at my first university, and I tested in algebra a year later. I guess that if you don't use it, you lose it. Or I drank my brain cells away in year 1 when living away from home. Either way, I knew that meant more classes. So I got involved in this program called Emerging Scholars, where you have your regular three-days-a-week math class and then take an additional "workshop" class where you work in small groups. I am not sure how *more* time in class sounded like a good idea, but I was in. And that is how I became a math teacher—well, sort of. It was a start.

I met a particularly amazing professor that changed my life in that program. I always liked math and helping other peers understand it, but I was also scared as hell of college math and didn't think I was good enough or smart enough to make it—a common theme, if you haven't noticed. He was the most charismatic, goofiest, happiest professor ever. Professors, historically, are too smart for their own good. They lack social skills and would rather be teaching a seminar to equally-as-smart people instead of twenty-something-year-old alcoholics. He had a way of teaching the basics that elevated the advanced. Over the next four years, he became a huge part of my life.

During that first summer, I had my first true teaching experience. Two professors led a program over the summer called Math Corps, a program hosted at Wayne State and open to students from seventh to twelfth grade in Detroit for free. It was brilliant. The whole philosophy was based on peer mentoring and feeding the program with past students who came back older and wiser. The seventh- to ninth-graders were "students," whereas the tenth- to twelfth-graders were the teachers (TAs, or teaching assistants). There were classes of ten to fifteen students in each group with three to four high school students, who were the leaders. There was also a college instructor who headed both the student and high school groups. They formed teams. The students took classes in mathematics, and so did the high school students.

The concept was developed by Steven Khan and Leonard Boehm in 1992, two mathematics professors at Wayne State who worked with inner-city youth when they weren't being badass professors. They recognized the injustice toward poverty-stricken kids in the city and wanted to make a difference. They will say that Math Corps was never about math and that it was about helping kids realize their own greatness and giving them a safe, fun place to learn and grow.

There were high expectations because that is a fact of life, and the kids were expected to rise to the occasion. And they did. You can't believe a kid is great and then not expect them to show their greatness.

These two professors and this program fueled my love for underprivileged kids, math, and teaching. I took this passion with me for my five years of teaching in Detroit charter high schools. The system was broken, the city was broken, and the people were even more broken. The kids either contributed to the mess, or they were victimized, fighting a never-ending battle to not be a stereotype.

So many sad stories stick in my mind, and I was helpless to fix them. (Remember when I said I want to fix, act, and do, do, do? Yep.) I tried, don't get me wrong. Within the four walls of my classroom, I tried to instill in each student the Math Corps values; and honestly, that was how I sincerely felt about them too.

I wanted to make math relatable and make myself relatable (and let's be honest: deep down, I felt broken and unworthy). I spent hours developing new and exciting lessons. I called the kids to check on them and make sure they were doing their homework. I brought food and left it in my drawer "in case someone was hungry." I sponsored class events, put on dances, organized car washes, arranged trips, helped girls get homecoming dresses, attended their sports games, and demanded the best efforts in class. I exhausted myself mentally and physically to make a difference. I hope I did. I know they certainly made a difference in my life.

I think about my students often. Some have made me proud, having stayed in school and out of trouble and made something of themselves in a world that is slated against them. Most overcame obstacles that no one should endure, child or adult: being born a crack baby; having both parents in prison; having both parents dead; watching a parent get murdered; being raped and molested by family members; having multiple friends and family members buried in the ground because of violence; having no running water at home; and never having a real bed, furniture, washer, dryer, or regular food. It makes me sick. But it opened my eyes to a world that I knew of but never experienced firsthand. It is all the grander when even just one makes it out and gives a big F U to the stereotypes and prejudice of the world.

It made me jaded to think that just ten miles north, the white suburbia schools had fields with AstroTurf, computer labs, tech centers, two gyms, auditoriums, and more than just football and basketball as sporting options, not to mention supportive families, heat in the winter, air conditioning in the summer, new clothes at Christmas, a meal on the table each night, a new car for their sixteenth birthday, and options for a world beyond high school. It is unfair, even repulsive, but nonetheless, it's a truth of our world.

I left one school and was teaching at a "suburban" high school near my home. I was eating in the teacher's lounge, listening to the "Woe is me" from other staff members and the "problems" they were having with kids or parents. I laughed to myself and then vomited in my mouth, thinking of how ignorant they sounded. It is easy to make a difference when the cards aren't stacked against you and your students, when they come to school clean, fed, and loved. Every teacher should have to do a stint in an inner-city school to appreciate their own personal circumstances and lifestyle and the union-based district they will be so happy to work in.

There have been many lessons in my life and many turning points that have molded my beliefs and passion. Teaching underprivileged youth is by far one of the biggest. To my friends that are still teaching, rock on with your bad selves. You are in the presence of greatness each day, looking into the eyes of our youth and molding their belief in themselves, for they all have greatness within them. It is up to us to help them harness it for good.

Your challenge

- What privilege do you have that you are taking for granted and could be more thankful for?
- In what way have you added sunshine to this world?

Part 3

HOW IT'S GOING

Being Born Again

*Out of these ashes
beauty will rise.*
—Steven Curtis Chapman

A birthday is the anniversary of someone's day of birth. I think giving birth to my babies was just as much my birthday as it was theirs. I became a completely different version of myself after entering parenthood. And I'm just getting started.

Before I was a mother to my own children, I had the incredible privilege of "stepmothering" a few special littles (and a puppy). It was partly harder leaving them than their dads. I learned a lot from them, but when people say, "Nothing prepares you for becoming a parent," they aren't joking, not in the slightest!

I think it is important for every woman to share and own their birth stories. So here are mine:

My first was born on a rainy, warm, September day. I felt my first twinge of a period cramp at 2:00 a.m., and another followed shortly after. I waited for a few more to occur to be sure I was really feeling what I was feeling before nudging my husband awake. He, of course, rolled over and said, "Didn't the midwife tell us to sleep awhile?" before nodding back off. It was about 5:30 a.m. when I told my husband he better get my stepdaughter over to his mom's house. While he was gone, I decided to call my mother. We talked for about forty-five minutes while I was quiet for a minute or so at a time, breathing through more and more intense feelings. Once my husband returned home, I got in the shower, and by this time, my contractions were making me stop and close my eyes to really breathe through them. But they'd pass, and I'd continue on. It was 9:00 a.m. when I checked in to triage and my doula arrived. The nurses couldn't find a vein to start my hep-lock, and it took three nurses before they called in the big guns to help. The last nurse blew out both of my hands, trying to get it in, and wouldn't you know? It fell out anyways. It was difficult to lie there while trying to be still for them. When checked by the nurse, I was over five centimeters dilated and in active labor.

I delivered in a hospital that had a special wing of six rooms dedicated to natural birth with more of a hotel than a hospital feel. I sank into the tub immediately and found a rhythm. There was a moment when I felt like I was going to be sick, but it was gone as fast as it came. In Michigan, you cannot deliver in a tub unless you are at home, so they drained the tub. But I desperately wanted to stay in that spot. I asked to stay there and just deliver in the empty tub, but they made me walk to the bed. Pushing was excruciating, and I could feel the "ring of fire" and a pop when he came out. I was shaking and trying to regain some sort of calm while they proceeded to stitch me up for almost an hour. I had no pain medication, so I felt every single numbing shot in my already exposed tissue.

Walking felt like a hundred pounds was going to fall out of my vagina at any moment, and I couldn't sit square on the toilet because the pressure was too much. I had a male nurse who I was leery of at first but ended up being such a blessing. He helped me pee for the first time while using the peri bottle on me. What a blessing he was. Jason was his name, and someone I will never forget. Nurses are another gift from the Almighty. Part of the reason I wanted an unmedicated birth was the sense of accomplishment it would bring. After years of physical fitness, I had trained my mind to overcome sensations in my body, and this would be the ultimate physical and emotional experience I could have. And that it was. The scariest thing was that I had no help. Yes, I had a team of doctors, a doula, and my husband; but ultimately, this was happening in *my* body. And no one, not even I, could stop it. It was about letting go of control—the control I have tried to have on my life since the beginning.

We named our son Phoenix, a fitting name for sure. In my past and in my husband's, there was fire, there was ash, and then there was *him*, this beautiful gift of a human.

Forty-eight hours after returning home, I passed a somewhat large blood clot and went to the doctor. I had been feeling like absolute crap, but wasn't that how you were supposed to feel after an eight-pound human just ripped you in half? I was clammy and white and had a headache while being examined. My midwife took some blood and told me that if the headache persisted through pain medication, to call.

I had been alternating Tylenol and Advil for the last couple of days as directed, but at 5:00 a.m. that next day, I still couldn't shake the headache. I called the on-call line, and the doctor looked up my lab results. She told me not to be alarmed but that I needed to go to the emergency room immediately. Don't be alarmed? Was that a joke? Good thing I hadn't even unpacked my bag yet.

When we arrived, my blood pressure was through the roof. Once again, the nurse couldn't get a vein, so I had to have some ultrasound-guided IV that was super deep in my upper bicep and couldn't bend my arm. On top of that, it was flu season, so the nurses told my husband to take my two-day-old baby and sit in the car, not in the dirty emergency room.

Long story short, I ended up with postpartum preeclampsia. I had zero blood pressure or swelling issues during my pregnancy, but I was learning quickly that this can happen up to six weeks later after birth. I was admitted and put on magnesium for twenty-four hours. Bedridden on a catheter, with nothing to eat or drink, I have never had such a bad headache in my life. Already exhausted from the most physically grueling experience of my life, I broke down in heaving tears. My husband had to hold my son up to my breast to nurse while I was in and out of being fully aware of what was happening. (Seriously, ladies, do *not* have a baby with a man that you cannot picture holding your baby up to your boob to nurse; trust me, you'll thank me later.)

After my stay, I was discharged with blood pressure medication and a strict "take it easy" order. I had to go back once a week for blood work to check my liver enzymes. My mother took me to every appointment because I still couldn't drive. How do people do this without help? I was hardly making it, and I had the best support system. I had made freezer meals in advance, I had a supportive husband, my mom came to help most every day, and I still couldn't turn my mind off enough to fully rest. You know how they say, "Sleep when the baby sleeps"? Yeah, that's horseshit. On top of that, I was feeding another human and setting my alarm to wake him up, terrified that he wasn't going to gain weight. The first twelve weeks of his life were likely the hardest time of my life.

Women do all this preparation for birth, but there is little postpartum support. I took the classes, did the reading, wrote my birth plan, visualized, and prayed on every detail. I decided on an unmedicated birth, hired a doula, and found a midwife/OB group, and then we were just sent home. When we were sent home the second time, I cried. I didn't want to leave the hospital. I didn't feel ready. I was so exhausted. Six weeks is too long after birth for a mother not to see a doctor. Mental health is so important, and so many mothers are *struggling* to keep it together. Insert society's view and expectations, and it's a wonder that more women aren't literally losing their shit left and right. Read this excerpt from Caylee Cresta I heard on Instagram.

> Don't worry, society expects enough from women. We're expected to age gracefully but never let ourselves go. Work like we have no children and parent like we have no job. They'll call the stay-at-home mother unfulfilled but the working mother selfish, although childless women are considered incomplete. Go chase that career but never at the expense of a family. Think like a man if you want to be successful but don't act like one if you want to be liked. We're supposed to mother our husbands but never treat them like children and put

out on demand but demand respect. Married and miserable is better than single and happy. But don't stay with an abusive man, but never break up your family. Don't marry a bum for love, but don't stay with a successful man for security. Don't be dependent on a man for money, but don't emasculate them by earning more. They'll tell us to embrace our sexuality but have some self-respect and to care about our appearance but stop looking for attention. Just say no but let them down easy. Be aware of your surroundings but stop being so dramatic. Practice self-love, but don't love yourself too much. Dream big but stay small, and would you like me to keep going?

I digress. Sorry, stay with me.

It eventually got better. I read some books, got a hang of a schedule, and found a balance. Between upping my meds and talking to Kaye for hours on end, I was getting into a groove and gaining confidence. I was still nursing, pumping, cooking, cleaning, and doing *all* the things. It was *a lot* and still is. I know you feel me, girl! Motherhood is not for the weak, that is for sure. And for someone like me, who has a deep-rooted coping mechanism of perfection and control, it makes it even harder.

As with so many things in life, you must trudge your way through it, and eventually, the pieces start to fall in place. We're never ready all the way. You will inevitably doubt yourself along the way, and sometimes you won't recognize yourself when you come out of the other end. There are days that I look in the mirror and think about how far I have come and all the things that have changed in just a few short years. I can look back now on the delivery of both of my children and say, "I did that." I also once again learned the lesson that what challenges us changes us. This time, it was for the better.

Your challenge

- What is a major life event that you feel changed you?
- What about it made the hard worth it?

$$\sim\!\!\diamond\!\!\sim$$

Overprepare, Then
Go with the Flow

You want to know what you're really made of? Have a kid. Having children tests your marriage, friendships, priorities, and coping skills. I was nervous when I found out I was pregnant with my second child. Would I tear again? I was still trying to feel "normal" after my first child, who was now a month shy of one and a half. Plot twist: A global pandemic was announced the week I found out I was pregnant. Cue the morning sickness, which was really all-the-time sickness, and uncertainty. And here I was, homeschooling my nine-year-old step-daughter and taking care of my very emotional toddler day in and day out. Who chooses this nonsense? If you do, no judgment. It is just beyond hard. It felt like Groundhog Day *every. Single. Day.*

This went on for a grueling three months—well, the sickness at least. The pandemic is still raging as I write this sentence. In that first two weeks, where I remember hearing on the news that the pandemic would be under control very shortly (haha), I went to Meijer while on the verge of projectile vomiting and snagged as many toys and activities as I could fit into two carts. If we were going to be locked up together, you better believe I was going to throw the kitchen sink at it. I figured that each new item would keep their attention for a whopping ten minutes, so if I bought twenty things, I'd have some entertainment for three hours and twenty minutes…*fuck*. This was going to be a long two weeks!

I felt more prepared for baby number 2. I understood my physical limits, and everything wasn't as new and scary. The unknown is still a thing no matter how many times you're pregnant. Insert a pandemic and horror stories I heard about some spouses testing positive and not being able to attend the birth. I panicked in a different way. This time I focused on creating an experience that I wanted, and I manifested that as much as I possibly could. With Phoenix, I didn't have as much time in the tub as I wanted, and tearing was a big concern. I was envisioning laboring in the shower this time and asked Kris if he wanted to be more involved because we weren't having a doula this time. He said, "No, thank you." Writing this, I can just hear God laughing at him and me and saying, "Just you wait."

I had been having Braxton-Hicks contractions, where your belly gets tight but there is no pain, all week leading up to delivery. I never had these types of contractions with Phoenix, so I was rolling with it. Once you surpass forty weeks, my midwife suggested a non-stress test where they hook up a monitor to your belly to make sure all is well with the baby. I was at that appointment Friday, November 20, and could see the contractions on the screen. She didn't check me because I wasn't in any pain. Come that evening, I was so over being pregnant that I went to bed, and the second I felt even a tinge of a cramp, I told myself I was in labor. Lo and behold, I guess I really was. I couldn't sleep and ended up waking Kris up at around 10:30 p.m. He called his mom, who arrived a little after 11:00 p.m. I had one moment when I was on the phone with my mom, told her I felt like I was going to throw up, and got all clammy. It passed, and I was having contractions for sure now. But I was doing well in between. They say to pay attention to what a woman does in between contractions. When I was in full-on labor with Phoenix, I was in my own world in between contractions. I was taking deep breaths, had my eyes closed, and was in the zone. With Keller, I was walking, talking, saying goodbye to Kris's mom, and hopping in the car. I put on my meditation in the car, and within seven minutes, I told Kris I needed to take my pants off. We were just getting on the expressway… He looked at me, and I felt the baby crowning. He said, "What do I do?" I instinctively said, "Call 911."

We were in the car a total of 12 minutes before our son was born. Kris pulled over on the side of the expressway and as he ran around to my side and threw open the door, I was telling him to catch him. Keller was on my chest, wide-eyed, staring at me before I knew it. Don't get me wrong, I was screaming in pain, but it got real so quickly that the only thing I could do was surrender.

Luckily, he was breathing and perfectly healthy. The cops and paramedics seemed more nervous than

I was. The paramedic's hands were shaking when they cut the umbilical cord. Long story short, the front seat of my Jeep needed a *deep* cleaning.

This experience is a metaphor for life; overprepare and then go with the flow. We can plan, prepare, and pray, but in the end, sometimes the experience isn't at all what we envisioned. Don't get me wrong, you should know by now that I am a *planner*. I want to know what's coming and be ready for every nuance. Inevitably, though, life will throw you into the deep end, and it's your job to learn how to swim. But preparation can serve as a life jacket—the savior that will keep your head above water while you adapt and surrender.

It is an experience that I will always look back upon in awe. My husband, the one who didn't want to be involved in the birth, was the first to touch our son. All my fears about how this labor would feel in comparison to my first, the physical trauma, and the recovery as well as the raging pandemic policies all ceased to exist at that moment. It also makes me realize how incredibly blessed we are that all went textbook good and that there were no complications with the delivery. There was quite a bit of physical trauma to my lady parts once again, especially with how fast he came, and I had to go back in for surgery six weeks after delivery.

Have you heard of pelvic floor therapy? If you haven't, you're not alone. I am surprised at how many women I have spoken to who also didn't know. It is quite literally physical therapy for your lady parts and pelvic region. Your vagina, butt, and pelvis are made up of muscles and tissue that also get fatigued and need stretching and strengthening just like every other muscle in your body. But this seems taboo to Americans because, number one, people are weird about openly discussing and caring for private parts and, number two, America doesn't emphasize post-partum care as much as other countries. Would you agree that birth is likely the most physically traumatic event that will happen in a woman's vaginal area? I concur. I was introduced to pelvic floor therapy by my sister. Surprise, surprise, she's always ahead of the medical game. I first went prior to having babies because I kept feeling like I had a bladder infection when I didn't. It was stress that was constantly flexing all my muscles, and I needed to *relax* them. Then after my epic spiderweb tear from having Phoenix, I was back in therapy. When I got pregnant with Keller, my priority was trying to prevent more damage. My whole pregnancy, I was in therapy. Ironically, the two ladies that spent an hour a week fingering me and making sure all my tissues were ready for stretch time became two of my favorite humans and friends. Shelley and Rachelle, I love you both and owe you so much. When it comes to your self-care, to your mental health, you have to be your own advocate. No one is going to do it for you. I'll end my soapbox with this excerpt from an article titled, "What Postpartum Care Looks Like around the World and Why the US Is Missing the Mark" written by Mandy Major and medically reviewed by Meredith Wallis, MS, APRN, CNM, IBCLC in 2020.

> Being the sole educator and provider of your postpartum care is not just hard. It's dangerous. Developed countries with the lowest maternal mortality rate consistently have one thing in common: routine check-ins at home.
>
> In Denmark, a midwife will call the day after discharge, and then an at-home health visitor will come to the house within 4 to 5 days.

In the Netherlands and Belgium, new mothers will have a kraamverzorgster, a maternity nurse who comes to the home to provide a minimum of 24 hours of care within the first 8 days after discharge.

For Swedish mothers, breastfeeding counseling is covered by insurance and midwives conduct as many home visits as needed within the first 4 days after delivery Trusted Source (with more visits available if needed).

Reardon points out France offers in-home postpartum care and all birthing parents automatically receive a referral for pelvic floor therapy.

It brings up a great point. Not only do we lack institutionalized support for birth, but America doesn't even treat it like other standard medical events. A knee replacement, for example,

> will warrant 1 to 2 nights in the
> hospital, 3 to 6 weeks at home
> with a specific rehabilitation
> timeline, and a rigorous course of
> physical therapy.

You guys, aside from the fact that I'd rather live in the above countries while having babies, I also wish maternity pay was better and recovery was taken more seriously by our society. Once I became a mother, these societal issues became glaring. Like most things, people don't care or see the urgency until they themselves are drowning in our system's inadequacies. Tell me if this is fucked up. My best friend lives in Ohio and works as a middle school teacher. She receives six weeks of 60 percent pay. Her husband, on the other hand, works for a large corporate company, and he receives four weeks *fully paid* time off to be at home with his wife and new baby. Although I am impressed a company actually honors paid time off for fathers, there should be no way in this entire world that the father gets more *fully paid* time off than the mother who is ripped from vagina to asshole from pushing an eight-to-ten pound baby out. How in the actual fuck is this a thing in America? In Sweden, new parents can take, at most, a one-year leave at 80 percent of their salary (De Vries et al. 2001). In Finland, mothers have the chance to take a one-year maternal leave supported by a state grant (Tarkka, Paunonen, and Laippala 1999).

Let's all move to Sweden or Finland and call it a day. Just kidding, but really, America needs to do better. Until then, keep pushing. Keep being your own advocate and show up for yourself. Surround yourself with a tribe that can help you where society doesn't.

Like everything, I got through it, and so can you. If you are struggling to find your inner strength, do something that scares the shit out of you. Or, as in my case, be forced to do something unimaginably hard both physically and mentally. It is in these experiences that we find out what we are made of. I had two babies with *no* drugs. When you make it to the other side of pain you can't run from, can't tap out on, or can't quit on, something purely magical lies on the other side. I wouldn't take back either of my birth experiences or any of my life's mental or physical challenges. They made me see life through a whole new lens. They made me a motherfucking boss. I always knew I was a force made of fire and grit, but the challenges I have faced have made me *un-fuck-with-me-able*. In those moments of doubt, reach back to these experiences and remember who the fuck you are.

Your challenge

- What is something you worked really hard preparing for and then it all went to shit and you had to take what life handed to you in a different way? Were you still happy you prepared for it? Did it help you "go with the flow?"
- What challenge in your life are you proud of yourself for getting through and overcoming? What new trait did it instill in you?

Dedication over Motivation

You want to know the secret of life? It is in what you do and think day in and day out. There. The end. I don't need to write any more. The 21/90 rule says it takes twenty-one days to form a habit and then continue it for another ninety days after that to make it become your normal cadence.

Want to know what matters to someone? Look at how they spend their money and how they spend their time. I've morphed into this person who strongly believes that planning isn't half the battle; it *is* the battle. Motivation runs out *quick*. That is where dedication comes in.

I spend a great deal of time on "healthy habits" (i.e., meal planning, meal prepping [these are not the same thing], physical fitness, mental decompression, stretching, eye cream, ingesting positive content, etc.) Self-care is what they call it. But I call it *living*. Properly caring for yourself, healing your past self, and creating a better today and tomorrow is what life is all about, folks. Your past self doesn't need you! But your future self certainly does.

There are days that are simply *hard*. You're tired emotionally and physically, and you don't want to do "it." Name your "it"—the dishes, the laundry, the phone call to the cable company, disciplining wild children, etc. I read somewhere that "any idiot can handle a crisis; it's the day-to-day that wears us out." You can't just show up on the good days. You must show up for your life *every* day. And that doesn't just mean physically showing up. I mean that you are a present *force* in your own life that moves the needle forward for yourself and your family. That is going to take mental and emotional presence and persistence from you.

So how, you may ask, does someone get there? Well, first, you gotta *want* it. Then you have to *work* for it. And lastly, you have to *keep going*. This is where my type A personality and OCD work for me. Once I set my mind to something, there is no stopping me. I will find a way. I will try my damnedest. Am I the most talented? Smartest? *Nope.* But I'll be the most hardworking. There will be setbacks. Expect them. Welcome the challenge. When in doubt, do the next right thing. Move the needle forward, and eventually, you'll be hitting your goals left and right.

The victim mentality is like quicksand, and soon enough, we have an inner monologue that screams, "You can't do it. She's got it together more than you. That's why she's so good at ___________!" Fill in the blank. *Lies!* No one has it together. People choose how they spend their time, and that showcases what they care about. Do some people have it harder than others? For sure! Do some people start behind the eight ball simply because of their upbringing? You bet! Does it mean you can't do something, be something, or have something? *Absolutely not!* It all starts with your mentality and your ability to be honest with yourself, where you are, and who you want to be.

Therapy gave me the ability to be very self-reflective and honest with myself even when I didn't want to be. There are still things in my past that I am coming to grips with, and I can now see my role in the madness. Time heals nothing unless you move along with it. And moving along with it means only looking back to learn. I spent a lot of time reliving my hurt to punish myself. That does nothing for my future! What are you dwelling on that you need to process and let go? What can you be more honest about with yourself so that you can grow from it?

I read this saying once that said, "Choose your hard. Marriage is hard. Divorce is hard. Choose your hard. Obesity is hard. Being fit is hard. Choose your hard. Being in debt is hard. Being financially disciplined is hard. Choose your hard. Communication is hard. Not communicating is hard. Choose your hard. Life is never easy. It will always be hard. But we can choose our hard. Pick wisely."

Whoa…read that again.

You want to change your life? Stop making excuses. You can be committed to your excuses, or you can be committed to change. But you can't have both. I guarantee you that there is someone busier than you that's hustling harder than you *right now*. People ask me how I stay so on top of things. My answer? I don't let myself fall behind. I do things *every single day* to move myself and my life forward in a way that I want it to look. I spend time processing my past to have a better future. I show up and be the best I can be for that day at that moment. Whatever you're not changing, you're choosing. That's the reality. So *want it*, *work for it*, and *keep going*.

Your challenge

- Think of one thing you want to see come to fruition in your life. Manifest that shit and then come up with *one* step you can take right now to start your journey.
- What can you be more honest about with yourself and the choices that got you to where you are now?

In Hindsight

*Life can only be understood
backwards, but it must
be lived forwards.*
                    —Soren Kierkegaard

I remember thinking that forty was so old and telling my mom that I wanted to have a baby at sixteen so I wouldn't be an "old mom." It's probably because I thought my mom just "didn't get it" when I was a tween. Jokes on me for that one. Now I look back and think, *Shit, I am three years to forty, and I don't feel old!* I mean, my joints do, but my mind doesn't! My friends are the leaders at their jobs. We have put in ten years of professional job time. My bestie just got a school principal position, and when she told me, I was like, "Holy shit, we're there!" We are the old people now that kids look at and think, *Adult.* It's strange and humbling to think that in my twenties, I was in a couple of serious relationships, lived on my own, and finished my bachelor's and master's degrees, but now, looking back, that was *so* long ago!

I don't even want to think about what fifty or even sixty is going to feel like! Now I understand when I ask my mom, "Who was your best friend in college or high school?" or "When did I start saying full sentences?" and she can't even remember—because it all blends together. And after a while, it is *so long ago.* It makes me realize that the things that are such a big deal at the moment are really blips on the life spectrum. *But* all the blips add up to this grand life of ours.

Some of the life events I have shared in this book seemed *so big* and overwhelming at the time. The amount to process is suffocating. With a lot of people, digesting and healing aren't completed in the moment or even the year that the event happens. Therefore, we must look back sometimes to move forward. Now, notice how I didn't say "*dwell* on the past" or "*live* in the past." I said "*visit* the past in a safe and healthy way." I advise you to do this with help from a professional. Sometimes, when we "look back" on our own, we can go down a rabbit hole and beat ourselves up instead of heal. I spent a lot of time doing that as well. When you look back through a different lens with the help of a professional, then real healing and transformation can occur. We can break cycles and habits that have held us back in our past lives. We can change our thoughts and behaviors at the moment, which, in turn, changes the trajectory of our future.

How many times have you let your past trauma, experience, and triggers dictate your thoughts and feelings in the present? How much of your current emotions are truly related to what's happening in the now and not bubbling up from the past? If you can take a moment to pause and ask yourself those questions at the moment, it will help you respond from an informed, readjusted place. *This is how we change the future.* This is how we grow through what we go through.

Growth never stems from a place of comfort. Get comfortable being uncomfortable. It means you're moving the needle *forward*. I am so grateful for every chapter of this book, every struggle, every experience, and every mistake that has taken me out of my comfort zone and made me *thrive*. I love all of myself now. Not all the time and not every minute of the day, though. There are seasons and moments when I have more self-doubt than others. But I have a *team* of ladies, a family who loves me, kids and a husband that depend on me, a job that is rewarding, hobbies that *fill up my* cup, and my inner badass to pick me up when I'm down. No one gets out of this alive. So I leave you with this:

> Life should not be a journey to the grave with the intention of arriving in a pretty and well-preserved body, but rather to skid in sideways in a cloud of smoke, thoroughly used up, totally worn out, and loudly proclaiming, "Wow, what a ride!" (Hunter S. Thompson)

Your final challenge

- What would you tell your younger self if you had a chance?
- What "mistakes" are you proud of because they made you grow into a better version of yourself?

- How can you make the rest of your days fulfilling and rewarding?

Things I would tell my younger self:

- Travel to another country. Study abroad, learn other cultures, and meet people unlike yourself.
- Make mistakes; you won't regret most of them. (*Done!*)
- Sadness isn't forever.
- Overthinking is not a waste of time; that is how we prepare and figure things out.
- Listen more to yourself. Most of the time, other people do not know the answer that is best for you.
- You are the main character of your story, so be unapologetically you.
- Consistency is the key to everything in life.
- Be your own best friend. Don't rely on other people to make you happy; they won't be able to.
- You don't have to be the best at something to do it. Outwork everyone in the room and take chances.
- Don't invest in people that don't invest in you. Relationships are a two-way street.

Conclusion

Remember when I said to find your tribe?

> May you attract someone who speaks your language, so you don't have to spend a lifetime translating your soul. (Nadin Saisir)

I would like to end this labor of love with a tribute to the humans who have made my existence worthwhile. These wonderful people have been by my side as my constant circle and are helping me row the boat of life. I hope they all read this, smile, and know just how thankful I am to know them and call them my tribe.

My parents must go first on this list, and I don't even think I can write about how much they mean to me. They are the two people who truly know who I am and who not only made me but also *made* me into the woman I am today. My mother—although referenced in previous chapters as, at times, calculated and cold—is also strong AF and doesn't sweat the small stuff. She doesn't get caught in the minutia of life and can let something roll right off her back. My favorite memories of my mom are when she would let me use her lipstick in the car and jamming out to California Raisins or Simon and Garfunkel. She also made every single one of my Halloween costumes by hand as well as my homecoming dress. I have vivid memories of her singing me to sleep. Mom, you know the song, *Lord of the Dance* and French braiding my hair for picture day. If I forgot a homework assignment at home, my mom came to my rescue. There was an afterschool snack and dinner on the table EVERY. SINGLE. NIGHT. I never missed a doctor's appointment, dentist appointment, summer camp, application deadline, or school project because of my mother. She volunteered at a homeless shelter at our church and took us with her. She volunteered at a hospital, made blankets for the homeless, and took us caroling at nursing homes during Christmas. Looking back now as a mother myself, I know how backbreaking parenthood is, and I didn't make it any easier on her. She has always been my advocate at school, with doctors, in sports, and everything in between. She's a lot like me and shows love through doing. She has literally become one of my favorite people, and I owe her the world for putting up with me and teaching me how to be a partner and parent.

My dad, well, if you know Jerry, you know how awesome he is. Jerry remembers our waiters' names, and if he meets you once, he will have your life story memorized. He is generous and hardworking and was always a very involved "girl" dad. He coached my junior powder-puff team, went to every dance competition and parent-teacher conference, and never missed a family meal. He also told me to change my clothes into something more appropriate, dragged me out of a party I wasn't supposed to be at, picked me up from jail after a DUI, and stayed up to wait when I didn't come home on prom night. I am so sorry for all the above transgressions. All things are what I dread as my own children grow up. My dad is also 100 percent Armenian, the first generation born in America. I am super proud to be a part of the Marsoupian family and have Armenian roots. He could always talk me down off a ledge without making me feel judged (I mean, unless he was really mad because I'm an idiot). He has taught me the importance of self-respect and being able to stand on my own two feet. I love you, Mom and Dad, and I thank you for seeing me through the hardest times and rooting for me at my best.

My first bestie is Kayeann Batanian. This special, special human has brought so much joy and peace to my life. The first day I met her, I was in my second year of teaching at a charter school in Detroit's west side. The previous year, I didn't even have a classroom. I rolled around all my teaching supplies on a cart each hour to a different room when that teacher had their prep hour. It was beyond crazy, stressful, and something my thirty-seven-year-old self could never do. She was now the unlucky teacher to have a cart, and she taught in my room in the last hour of the day, which was my prep hour. I hated it. I wanted some peace and quiet, but instead, she had a pack full of unruly freshmen to teach science to. On top of all that, the thermostat never worked in my room, and it was always a sweltering ninety degrees. One day, she approached my desk, where I was trying to focus on lesson plans. She leaned over to me and said, "It's hot as balls in this room." I laughed and immediately loved her. She could hold her own with the kids and had the "take no shit" attitude you need to survive in an urban school.

In our second year of teaching together, we were supposed to move into a brand-new building, but, of course, construction was behind. But we had already cleared out all our furniture and supplies from our current building. Therefore, we started school with no student desks or supplies. With increased enrollment, we didn't even have room for the ninth graders to be in our old building, so the school decided to rent a community center building a couple of blocks away for us to utilize in the interim. No joke, this building had no air and was a complete dumpster, and every morning, the three ninth-grade teachers had to walk their students down the block and spend the day trying to conduct learning. I *cannot imagine* the uproar this would have caused in a middle-class district north of the city. It was horrible. That was the year we both carried our heaviest weights and drinking the stress away.

From there, our friendship grew organically. Once we moved into the new building, we found that her classroom was right at the top of the large entryway stairs. She taught freshman science, and sometimes her class size was up to thirty-eight students. How in the world are you supposed to teach in that environment? She rocked it, though. She has an uncanny ability to sift through the bullshit and focus on what is in her control. Even now, as a mom to two beautiful babies, she doesn't sweat the small stuff.

After our first year there, she left and moved to another district, and I also left in search of a new teaching job shortly after. We have maintained a long-distance relationship for over eleven years. I have spoken to her every single day in one way or another since the day I met her—except during her ten-day honeymoon. I tried to leave her alone without having a breakdown. She knows all my deep, dark secrets, and if she ever batted an eye at them, I could never tell. If I had to choose one person to live on a deserted island with, I would choose her. I don't know if we would survive, but I know we'd go out laughing and loving each other.

Andrea is my ride-or-die. We survived all of our twenties and now most of our thirties side by side, cheering each other on. I met Andrea in the most hilarious way. We met in our second year of college after both attending other universities for our freshman years and then moving home to attend our inner-city commuter college. So here we were, unknowingly sharing a similar past year, waiting outside our classroom for the first day of class, standing across the hallway from each other. In struts the *hottest* guy, passing between us. We both stared at him and then locked eyes with each other, grinning as we chuckled. From that day on, we have been best friends.

She was the maid of honor at my wedding; helped me move about six times; was my date to weddings; and renewed my confidence after losing jobs, failing interviews, and kissing one hundred frogs. She attended my boyfriend's funeral, planned a surprise thirtieth birthday party for me, and had an *unwavering* sense of love and loyalty. She is truly the *sun* in a sometimes-dark world.

She and Kaye gave me the greatest gift: a recording of them saying affirmations for me to listen to when I was in labor. They are the voices that I want to hear in my most challenging moments. She calms and centers me when I cannot focus. She has seen me at my worst and pushed me to be my best. She would be my first phone call if I needed a getaway driver, that's fo sho!

Next up is my lovely Melissa. We grew up in the same city, but we went to different high schools. We reconnected later in life as teachers in another inner-city school. Coincidentally, she taught at the same school Andrea did, and I ended up joining them in year three of teaching. The three of us seamlessly intertwined. I will say that working with your tribe is so fulfilling! I not only experienced them person-ally but professionally. So here we were, three women trying to make a difference with all odds against us. That made me fall in love with Melissa even more. She was and still is a fantastic teacher and such a steady, grounded person.

I trust her to keep what I say private. Whenever I talk to her about a problem I am having, she asks all the right questions to guide me in the right way instead of just telling me the answer! This, my friends, is a gift. Get yourself someone like Melissa. We discuss books, cooking, and organizational prac-tices, and she was who I chose to be my birth partner if my husband couldn't be there. She is logical and steadfast. She is my rock and would give me confi-dence because she has confidence in me.

When Melissa was going through a tough life transition, I was so happy to be by her side to help her navigate that chapter and it made us closer. I have seen her grow into a more confident, independent version of herself over the years. I love you, girl, and I look forward to being old AF and going to the mov-ies with you!

Next up is my sister, Allison. We have been opposites since I entered this world four years and one day after she was born. Where she was smart, rational, and responsible, I was (also smart) ground-less and rebellious. She always knew what she wanted and where she was headed, while I, on the other hand, wavered in my decisions and was often misguided.

We were never the typically close sisters, but we always were just that—sisters who were there for each other no matter what. Have you ever been in the same room with someone and just feel better sim-ply because they are there? That's how I feel about her. One piece of silver lining during the pandemic is that we grew closer because literally everyone just stuck to seeing their immediate family members, and lucky for her, I was it. As adults now, both married with children, we can relate on another level, and it has been great, getting to know her as such.

I know that when growing up, she tried to sup-port me despite not quite understanding me, and I respect that now. I didn't even understand myself. I am pretty sure that despite our four-year age differ-ence, I lost my virginity before her and made about one hundred poor decisions before she ever made one. She graduated third in her class from high school and from college with honors. She got me a card once about taking the road less traveled. That was the best "agree to disagree" card I've ever gotten. And it also made me think that maybe she was proud that I forged my own path. (I also have a tattoo of this.)

Once I got into high school, I felt like an only child because she was away at college. But I remember sleeping in her bed when she left because the sheets smelled like her. She's the only one who would recognize our mom's old dishes or be able to talk about that vacation when we were young. I also remember always wanting to be around her. I wanted to play with her dolls, dress in her clothes, and sleep in her room on Christmas Eve.

I have learned so much from her. She is insanely intelligent and very emotionally and physically aware. She sees things in black and white, whereas I get caught in the gray. There is something intangible about sharing flesh and blood with someone that binds you together, and I'm proud to call her my sister.

Here comes my brother from another mother, Eric. Eric and I met when I was nineteen and he was eighteen. It was my second year of college, and I was now home and commuting to school. In my attempts of meeting new people, I was invited by a football team member to a house party in a nearby town. I enlisted my high school girlfriends to come with me over Thanksgiving break. Because who goes to a random house with random dudes alone? You know, trying to be smart. That was the night I met Eric, the most charismatic in the group. From that night, for the last eighteen years, we have been friends. We dated for a short time but landed on friends instead shortly thereafter.

We have been through all of life's phases together. He went into the Army not long after we met and onto ranger school. I wrote him, I sent him care packages, and we messaged on Myspace (ugh, Myspace, how hilarious). He has had girlfriends (and now a wonderful wife), and I have had boyfriends. And one standard I always kept was that if they don't get along with Eric, then I can't date them. When he met my husband, I was nervous because they both have alpha personalities, and Eric can be somewhat "spicy," if that's even a good word for it. But they got along, and he ended up standing up at our wedding, which I have always wanted.

Eric has shown up for me countless times. He was my date to a wedding when I was going through a hard breakup with Mr. Cheater. He helped me paint and move in and out of multiple houses. He came to my ten-year high school reunion. He dragged me out when my boyfriend died and protected me from weirdos. He makes me feel protected and confident, and it is always a good time when he's around. He tells me like it is, and we don't always agree. But he accepts me 100 percent for who I am, mistakes and all. He would bail me out of jail if I needed him to (which has happened, but I couldn't remember his phone number!). I also know that he would physically punch someone in the face for me, and even though he'd likely be late, he'd always show up for me.

I saved the best for last: my husband, Kris. I kind of love that I even have a *husband* because I spent a lot of my life feeling unlovable. I met Kris through a work friend, and we were set up to meet as she invited us both over for dinner. The first thing I noticed about him was his super sexy deep voice and nice beard! We had a great night, playing Cards Against Humanity and laughing. He respectfully texted me later that evening, saying it was nice to meet me and to drive safe home. I didn't reach back out to him for a couple of weeks, but when I did, he was quick to say yes to a dinner date. I found him hard to read and quiet but also observant and dominant. We dated just about a year before I was pregnant and were engaged shortly after. We got married at the courthouse when I was six months pregnant with Phoenix.

He has given me the best gifts in my life: my two perfect sons. Moments after I delivered Phoenix, I looked up at him and thanked him for making this precious bundle that was lying on my chest. He has worked his ass off to crawl his way out of his own past decisions and make a better life for himself and his daughter. I respect the shit out of him for that. If I'm being honest, the darkest parts of him are the ones I love the most.

When I came into the picture, he was five years sober and working a minimum-wage job to work his way up. Now, five years later, he is doing what he loves with his best friend and business partner, and we are working as a team to thrive financially and emotionally as a couple.

I am so proud of him, and I am so proud of us. It is not easy being a true partner to someone else. It is not easy parenting small humans and coordinating the daily grind with someone. But as every other chapter in this book clearly states, I am not interested in easy. I am interested in worth it. Thank you, babe, for being someone I can laugh with and who is committed to this crazy life beside me and for making life with you worth it.

If you haven't told your tribe that they are, in fact, your tribe, then I recommend you stop reading and go do it! Life is too short to not show appreciation and return the favor. Write the letter, leave the voice mail, and make it weird because these people, the tribe you were born into and the one you chose, are the most important relationships of your life. I encourage you to look back at all the people who have made a big impact on your life—people who have sustained the storms, caused the storms, taught you love, and helped you heal—and reflect on those memories. Then tell the good ones how appreciated they are.

Here are books that I highly recommend. These have all influenced my journey:

- *Captivating: Unveiling the Mystery of a Woman's Soul* by John and Stasi Eldredge is amazing. I have read this book about ten times. I swear I learn something new each time depending on where I am in my life. There is another book written by John Eldredge titled *Wild at Heart*, and it is for men.
- *You Are a Badass: How to Stop Doubting Your Greatness and Start Living an Awesome Life* by Jen Sincero. I mean, seriously, I couldn't come up with a better title myself. If you

are looking for a good, worthwhile kick in the pants, this is a great place to start!

- *The Girl with the Lower Back Tattoo* by Amy Schumer. This chic rules, and the personal-essay style she writes in inspired me to write my own story.
- *God Never Blinks: 50 Lessons for Life's Little Detours* by Regina Brett. Regina is a breast cancer survivor and writer for Ohio's largest newspaper. She has other books, and I have read them all. I encourage you to do the same.
- *Natural Hospital Birth: The Best of Both Worlds* by Cynthia Gabriel. This book was my bible when I was pregnant with my first son and changed my view drastically. It provided me with the necessary guidance and education I needed to make my own informed decisions.
- *A Million Little Pieces* by James Frey. If you have known anyone who struggles with addiction, this book pulls at every humanistic bone in your body. It is skillfully written and one of my all-time favorite novels.

Acknowledgments

I am so grateful to all the people reading this book, laughing along with me, and finding solace in my story. To all the people who have inspired and pushed me to write my story, thank you for loving me. To my parents, who have been my rock and safety net, and to my girls, who are my absolute saviors in this life, thank you for accepting all of me in all my forms. To my husband, who gave me the gift of my beautiful children and grinds with me day in and day out. To the universe for placing people and circumstances in my life that have given me the ability to grow through what I go through.

Everyone has their own story to tell, and it should be shared with dignity and pride no matter the hiccups it took to make you who you are. You are the sum of all your decisions; good and bad, they are equally important. Don't ever forget that. Forward is forward no matter how slow. Forge your own way on your own terms. There are no practice rounds. This is the main event, folks. You're in it!

About the Author

Laura is currently living with her husband and three children—Harlow, Phoenix, and Keller—in Michigan. She has a bachelor's degree in mathematics from Wayne State University and earned her master's degree from Concordia University in curriculum and instruction and educational leadership. She enjoys cooking and making traditional recipes with a healthier twist. She is ferociously passionate about motivating others to live with purpose and accept themselves for all that they are. *Trial and (Mostly) Error* is Laura's first book.

You may reach her via Facebook (facebook.com/laura.nicole143) or Instagram (instagram.com/_laura143/).

www.ingramcontent.com/pod-product-compliance
Lightning Source LLC
Chambersburg PA
CBHW061347160726
47995CB00001B/208